The Cartographer's Lament

Also by Dennis Phillips:

POETRY
Sonnets (Magra Books, 2022)
17 Meditations on Time (Magra Books, 2021)
Mappa Mundi (Tailsman House Publishers, 2019)
Desert Sequence (Magra Books, 2016)
On Rooks (Ninja Press, 2015)
Measures (Talisman House Publishers, 2013)
Mapping Stone (Post Media Books/Otis Books/Seismicity
    Editions, 2013)
Sophia's Laments (Ninja Press, 2012)
Navigation: Selected Poems 1985–2010 (Otis Books/Seismicity
    Editions, 2011)
Study for the Possibility of Hope (Pie in the Sky Press, 2010)
Sand (Green Integer, 2002)
Study for the Ideal City (Seeing Eye Books, 1999)
Credence (Sun and Moon Press, 1996)
Book of Hours (ML NLF, 1996)
Twenty Questions (Jawbone Press, 1996)
Means (Parenthesis Writing Series, 1991)
Arena (Sun and Moon Press, 1991)
A World (Sun and Moon Press, 1989)
The Hero Is Nothing (Kajun Books, 1985)

FICTION
Hope (Green Integer, 2007)

TRANSLATIONS
More Fugues by Susanna Rabitti (Co-translator Paul Vangelisti;
    Magra Books, 2019)
Mechanical Love by Milli Graffi (Magra Books, 2018)
Fugues by Susanna Rabitti (Co-translator Paul Vangelisti;
    Magra Books, 2018)

EDITIONS
Nausikaa's Isle (Postmedia Books, 2015)
Joyce on Ibsen (Sun and Moon Press, 1999)

The Cartographer's Lament

Mappa Mundi, ii

Dennis Phillips

Magra Books

LOS ANGELES – BAGNONE

2025

Design by River Jukes-Hudson

Cover art by Courtney Gregg

In 2021 Magra Books published "17 Meditations on Time," reprinted herein, as no. 15 in its chapbook series. Following its debut in 2016, the series culminated with volume 29 at the start of this year. Magra is now publishing longer, perfect-bound books, of which *The Cartographer's Lament* is the first.

Order from IngramSpark and www.magrabooks.com

S.E. Pessin & Paul Vangelisti, editors

ISBN 979-8-9926955-2-6

magrabooks.com
magrabooks@gmail.com

PRINTED IN THE USA

For

Courtney & Sophia

CONTENTS

And the sun high over horizon hidden in cloud bank
lit saffron the cloud ridge
                    dove sta memora

Ezra Pound, CANTO LXXVI

Apostrophe

1

Of holidays and rituals; of records kept;
of distinguishing signal from noise;
of doling out what's dole-able;
of highways and light torrents;
of time and space combining
as we understand them to combine;
of the physical, actual impediments
we must confront to get to B.

Of the witnesses—or agents—
be they you or those we call they.

*

Damp sun angles off leaves and pavements.
Pre-winter light from the south.

The world falls apart
and all we conjure's weather.

O, transparent messenger[1]
tangible in evocation
and then not tangible at all.

Of pressure and compression.
A meteorology of steam.

*

Gradually the stream comes into focus.[2]
And speaking of intangibles
though leaves drop at the approach of solstice—
latitude being what it is—
voices braid and unbraid floating just beyond
until retrieved—plucked really—
to bind to something else made of sound.

---

1   Tilted meridian, rivers of atmosphere, longitudes ribboned,
the wanderer wound in weather.
2   By stream I may have meant time and seeing it—or part of it—
as a whole flowing fabric, the mistake we make as locals.

And the voices sometimes attach to
but are always separate from
faces and bodies, from shadows sorting shadows.

*

Traces of winter light:
percussions, refractions, incidental angles,
bounced off the shed rails of the city,
the covered deserts, the islands off the coast.

Winter's trace lodged in shadows
in the obliquity of shadows
in shadows of shadows.
Concussions and recapitulations,
pavements soaked and dried,
native habits. Magnified. Repeated.

2

Dark morning damp
as ere beneath a waning moon
demon sky, early glimpse of color
as the blanks fill in.

Above, roiling cloud and cries
of birds too high up in the current.

The world flees us
and all we conjure's weather.

This the basin, arroyo seco,
ridged by pressures that insist on the desert's cryptography.

Il pianto d'Ariana a different key of abandonment,
the labyrinth escaped easier to understand
than the labyrinth of pressures and currents.

Ariadne betrayed resolves into Locatelli's suite
more organized, more harmonious
than anyone's idea of chaos.

It's that, at the mouth of the labyrinth,
one's search for string compounds urgency.[3]

You can't live in the counterpoints,
can't live in the thing made of words.

---

3   Spin, measure, cut. Spin, measure, cut.

3

Death doldrums and humid air
sleep an uneasy rival
though airplanes intervene, and flights of other sorts.
Dim unburied memories that rebury at dawn
and still you hide your signal
in the architectures of noise.

4

Your entrances and exits in the shadows of pages
no more dream-like than the landscapes you keep moving
from city to desert to island to ocean.

Who can trust the shadows or the umbra's red darkness
when your caprice turns them to contraries?

You laugh at the idea of thought
and I can't blame you.
(So much for schedules.)

I know you're listening and doubt it,
and who you are, and why I'd address you
if I knew.

More than landscape and weather
you're not unlike virtue, hope, or gravity.

But why is it that when you show up
a pressure wave of words precedes you?

Words that effloresce and images too
and harmonies that move like tides
flooding and neaping.

I need to believe you're the other half of this voice,
the necessary catalyst to complete the contract.[4]

At a different time or with a different person
might this whole thing—or you—
simply have been called prayer?

---

4   I take a breath from you confused. A rest? A theft? You respond
by not responding. Is that as I wish it?

Seventeen Meditations on Time

Preface

Tiny bird pecking high above.
Behind, a flying insect strikes a window.
A black ant crawls on a white vinyl chair adjacent.
Circumjacent, oak leaf and acorn occasionally fall.

The red-capped bird is black and grey and white.
Others join and then the pecking stops.
Spanish moss hangs from oak boughs.
The air is still.

Earlier a large doe lay in a circle of sunlight.

A slight breeze commences.
Insects vanish. The deer is gone.
Boughs and mosses sway.

A chime sounds
and because I'm using language
I know that I'm awake.

1

Sudden early light as a year ago,
light that erases margins,
now as then.

The chariot and its passengers, jetted or wingèd,
the golden light or argent,
things gained or lost or never possessed.

There's also that walking shadow
perhaps aging gum inside the eye.
For sure nothing magic unless by magic
we understand the workings of metaphor.
In that case the chariot casts an umbra
and if that be true then right now
the penumbra's a golden thing,
annular. As a year ago.[5]

---

5   Hot autumn morning. It may be my birthday but the fish need to
eat. And I, caught between wonder and irony, clear the gutters, do what needs
to be done, frustrated at the trivia of trivial things, bewildered at their gravity.

2

Wind clicks two points north and the sun slides south.

The force of another tongue,
its imprint of image and syntax
slides too, on a different scale.

Things fall away.

One pictures oceans and the arc of transpolar travel
where distance is rendered as interval.

Time the trickiest scale.
Its elements not what they seem.

Because one thing *models* another
it's not metaphor it's mirror.[6]
A mirror up to nature as a certain young man once said
himself a model or metaphor or mirror.

Cloud congeals in clear dark air.
Things fall away.

But first a grayscale cap of cloud erases a ridgetop[7]
and beside it funnels filtered light so another ridgeline
crenellated with the silhouettes of trees
is clear and flat and for some unknown reason
sublime.

---

6   Picking out common threads and braiding them is a rope
maker's art, the blue smoke of hemp, taut shrouds looped around
a loggerhead expressing a last bead of moisture, the strain and friction of
a captured thing, smoky incense rising.
7   For a while the room's aromatic and soon enough smoke,
like dust, settles on the generalized surface of things.

3

And if you find that the birds too high in the current
are shadows on your retina
or the distant sirens, mechanical or divine
just the ringing in your ears?[8]

---

[8]   ...which conjures so many illusions and why not subscribe?
What's not a retinal or walking shadow? Fog beshrouded morning cannot
blanket birdsong, sirensong, earsong.

4

I know you're listening and doubt it
and who you are and why I'd address you
if I knew.

You're more than landscape and weather
and not unlike virtue, hope, or gravity.

Certain words effloresce and images too,
certain lines move like tides
flooding and receding
but you're more than a debris line.

You may not be the one filled me with wonder.
You may not be the one to share it with me.
But you are the one I come to,
to the porch of a hidden cottage
beyond which I know I'm not allowed.

For sure you're the other half of this
the necessary catalyst to complete the contract.

5

Old father mid water column
hovering in blue abyss
a permanent version of the transitory
waving up from below
suspended[9]

---

[9]   A current not an arc, a measure, a gauge, a shepherd
of the actual.

6   *(After Crosson)*

Whiles yet the cool and temperate currents outlast the sun's track
and peace rests in the fold of an unsewn sheet
and all ideas fly free like birds from a Buddha's mouth,
especially the dogs.[10]

---

10   Everyone seems old. Especially the view. Especially the ocean.
Don't blame me for the syllables I count or the music I scavenge.

7

Weaving and reweaving
from a storeroom of thread.
Spin. Measure. Cut.

8

You go to sleep.
You awaken.
Before you verbs and Russians
array as colors on a wheel.
Gulls cry far above.

You know you're awake
and memory's the anchor.
Still, a shotgun in the closet,
pamphlets in a drawer,
debt and purpose,
blood on fingertips,
proof that neither color nor sound
recollect exactly why the lover
turns on the beloved.

9

And Odysseus again back in his palace
the trap set and the goddess beside him.
Pasadena summer hotter than ever
the very idea of time, baked and fleeting.

The trap set and the goddess presiding
or choose the fantasy that comforts
the immutable idea of time, running ahead
as missives from the east add to the jeopardy.

Or take comforts and fantasies as they come
Pasadena summer hotter but predictable
as missives from the east hold promise and yet
Odysseus returns once more to his palace.

10

The tides pull in and out.
Books are made of leaves.

Cataloging leaves are biologists and librarians.

Bar graphs also track, record and predict the tides.

Here the reflection becomes strained
by and with and through time.

Dust collects despite us.
Air sustains more than we can see.
Hence Mt. Tambora, April 10, 1815, explodes,
biggest ever recorded, spread dust
three years around the globe
brought blizzards to summer
caused Mary Shelley to write her book, some say,
others that vampires appeared.

Leaves also cover ground.

Imagine a stratum of dead leaves
circling the troposphere.
Imagine a stratum of books there.

11 *Three-part Invention*

The poet walks out to his night office.

Odysseus back in place.
Akhilleus before the gates of a city.
Stephen bereft of his tower.
Lizzy acknowledged universally.

There is no time.

In dark windows the poet older
the world still young
and three young women lithe and causal
at work on their project
frozen in memory.

Index and clock, the poet.

Spin, measure, cut.

*

The poet arrives phonemes afire,
can't tell the difference between
repetition and process.

Once the daughter across the table, on the floor.
Now the daughter makes the table.

*

The poet steps onto the porch
the sun not yet risen, the sky orange then gold.
Who voices the steps, we, not he, ask,
and notes scrapped and loose
flurry around the headwaters
of nothing more than this.

12

They say that *ontogeny recapitulates phylogeny*'s no longer valid.
What can it mean, that, like Freud, it keeps a literary value?

And so the old woman who defenestrates her granddaughter's doll
and appears in the granddaughter's granddaughter's dream
has a malevolent and benevolent face,
becomes a fiber in the paper of a map.

13

And who off to the desert now

      rolling tape of road
      mountains clear in the distance

And a motel room
and the smell of leaking stove

      boulders aggregated to foothills
      the sky black but warm

Like gold to airy thinesse beate

      what her skin will feel, her eyes see

14

The cartographer takes a place at the rail.
Early summer doldrums.

Looking up at a vortex of dark and rainless clouds,
sweating in crepuscular heat,
the cartographer charts the moment
as chicken singes on a grill
and the moment's elements
stand as units
to be arranged or omitted.

15

This is the part where the tent seems too small
and the illusion that seemed a lover
expands, fills the space,
becomes a force too great to overcome.

You might be Anchises, tricked by the gods into love
or poor Peleus, also fooled.
Or you may have no provenance at all
simply a juggler, ignorant of physics,
spinning so many plates on so many sticks.

This is the part where you let the plates crash
where you stop jacking the sticks.
You might be surprised:
the plates just might stay balanced.
You might discover it has nothing to do with you.

16

Finger the seam
stroke the fold.

Ants, mandibles cargoed, line the atom trail.
Ants invented the atom trail.

Pigs scream in the background.
Crows sail among hemlock.

Camped in the trees and observing the glade
we can't predict how the folds will open
or the seams hold.

17

The cartographer makes the map once more.

The scale is different every time,
land masses shift, rivers and mountains
arise or erase.

The work is never complete,
the charts are never quite right.

In the end, says the cartographer,
even taken together, the whole will be incomplete.
That is my vocation.

Foothills

1

At the base of steep mountains my north flank's protected. Sometimes location frees one from worry. But, orographically speaking, downpours can be quite destructive. Vigilance is necessary for rebounds of different sorts. Torrents of mud for example. Or sound.

In hot weather the range can appear even closer than it is, especially when the air is dry.

Other times I wait in deep shade and note my locale.

2

In summer ice doesn't melt but wait, that's a poem read at the base of steep mountains. When they write about sunrise, do they think of horizons 7000 feet above a valley's floor?

3

At the foot of a mountain wall clouds drape the ridges. Orographic.
And yet it's warm. This the world we live in now.

Atoms to atoms, butter for fish.

How did I get here, asks the monk. *My heart is not like yours*,
he says. Yet pressures build against the wall, mountains subducted up,
rain contracted down.[11]

---

11   Rats in the ivy, *spiders in the palm trees* hiding in the cracks.
The biome is working. On this thin crust, pushed up against a wall of steep
mountains, politics refract and rebound in increments too fine for the
actors to notice.

4

A front moves over the valleys
stops against a mountain wall.
The basin floods with light.

Take a path and leave well enough alone.

5

Why, then, do the dreams dissolve
as heat returns and monsoonal flow?
The old cartographer seeks to cleanse fingers of ink.
The room fills with Handel, moving air,
and the sounds of another's biography.

September begins to take on other meanings
and this not without a struggle
to belay the avalanche of distractions
nipping at one or another set of heels.

More and more the cartographer
seeks to map footprints, resting places,
the compression of earth where wheels once rolled.

Says the cartographer,
ask someone else if you need directions.

Desert Resequenced

1

Then came upon a terraced city
peopled by phantoms, night yet day
where, gather as you may and leave if you must,
your return will forfeit all you've collected.

The high road returning
returns through a land emptied of horses and people.

A guide comes out to meet you
equally puzzled as to why you're here
and where the others have gone.

2

Waiting for an emissary the world's full of emissaries waiting for
a story instead and the emissary or insects lighter than air, coral
insects heavy with depth each atmosphere a column weighing down
the messengers, the messages squeezed thin and indecipherable to
airy thinnesse squeezed.

Waiting for the currents to lift them too high in the currents, tiny
birds the emissaries in circuit too high in the circus, too high in the
story instead.

3   *Anabasis*

And Akhilleus who never enters the city
and the rock, sand, tracts of desert
of which the city is made, to which the city returns.

And then ocean slam against desert
in quarters so hostile to the city's roots
we come to entangle in their extremities.

Anabasis. Sand over sea. Sea over sand.
A ship seen above the top of dunes.

Once thought: "anabasis despite departure"
yet Akhilleus, who never enters the city,
we imagine entangled in extremities.

Stemming Lethe's current
last of five rivers to ford
in light filtered of shadows yet abundant of shade.
Katabasis from her shore downward
from whose erasure no traveler returns.

A great sphere of circulating birds
too high up in the currents
each a sign, each an agent.

4

Littered pavements
copper light
birds singing for hours.

5

And who off to the desert now.

> Motel room
> smell of leaking stove.

What her skin will feel, her eyes see.

> Boulders aggregated to foothills
> the sky black but warm.

Rolling tape of road
mountains clear in the distance.

6

Excrescence and efflorescence,
building, flowering, budding,
branching, leafing, the zygotes,
the meiosis and mitosis, the gestating, the yielding
and the desiccation, the browning, the dying away
and everything again blossoming.

You may not be the one filled me with wonder.
You may not be the one to share it with me.
But you are the one I come to,
to the porch of your hidden cottage
the one that dissolves the moment I see it.

7

Temperature cools
winds pick up
and we're left to wonder
about the tracks we've left.

Childhood, or Ten Fragments on Memory

1

Cartographer in the wheelhouse chartless.
On the floor ants march in topographic contours.
Are they the map?

Light fades.
Ants now few and far between,
wayward, random, searching for home.

This isn't childhood, isn't history,
isn't the dream of flying the labyrinth.

The map's in motion, lines shifting.
The polis, like memory, arises without a guide.

2

Maybe the point's turbulence in a turboprop
on a night flight to the desert or the morning flight
in a Beechcraft Bonanza returning in time for school
and that witnessing the clouds and their duneshadows from above's
an indication of a mystery we put ourselves in the midst of.

Sugar and almonds, coffee and Tang,[12]
even then astronauts circled far above the currents,
far above the birds, above the shell of air,
so high the ocean's depth concealed by dazzled surface
blue beneath atmosphere's thin veneer.

But they must have known
that all those sparks of starlight
crowding the black sky
are nothing but time long passed
finally reaching a receptor.[13]

Our atoms, our cosmos, our tiny birds
too high up in the currents.[14]

---

12   Motel room. Smell of leaking stove. Boulders aggregate to
foothills, night sky black but warm. In a pavilion near the pool, warm wind,
and memories unfurl.
13   The earth is not a metaphor, or a background on rollers.
14   What can it mean, that like Freud, *ontogeny recapitulates
phylogeny* keeps a literary value? And so the old woman with a malevolent and
benevolent face, who defenestrates her granddaughter's doll and appears in the
granddaughter's granddaughter's dream, becomes a fiber in the paper of a map.

3

Where the headwaters' capillaries narrow to a cell's breadth
and what courses isn't water or blood but voice
and the memory of voice, voice that can't hear itself
but flips disc by disc through its tiny sluice.

Pinned we are to memory, memory pinned to voice.

And what's called necessity we grapple up stuck in time.
Sometimes it seems to speak.
Sometimes a small boy in a cul-de-sac can hear it.

4

What if air and water were so close
in temperature and stillness
that moving between them was unnoticeable
but for the buoyancy?

And up the cove, emerging, standing,
palms on one shore, pines on another,
suddenly weight, feet on mantle, mantle on shoulders,
mantle over hearth in cave or house or hovel,
isolate or crowded, near or far from the city;
released from or weighted by the polis
that is, order and the keeping of order
and if absent, remade even as you cast your first steps in plaster
to remember, to record, to stop time.

5

Swimming far from shore
until the wind comes up
and the warm currents strong.

6

Full bower and bower's a house
a refuge an annex and in the end
made of leaves and twigs.

Who arrives and in what condition
secondary to what they arrive to.

And yet music sets the scene
and by scene picture a desert
and by desert picture buildings
some of masonry, some of wood,
some of branches, leaves and twigs.

Clouds cast shadows on dunes.

One summer leads to the next
and still the bower, fugitive, flimsy
poised to blow away.

7

The daughter far from home
the world she sees, the atmospheres she feels,
her father fixed in place
searching for the card he's holding.

The movement tests the past
where the world is shed of its randomness
and cards float up to screen
considered, used or ignored.

Each thing imagined. Each card an island.[15]

---

15   Taste the vector, in this case plumbs. And morning light on
bouldered hills. Sight and touch the vectors. That I've said this before, somewhere
between narrative and autobiography. No ideas but in specifics. Ants.

8

Summer light, early through east curtains[16]
hot through closed windows
hot across knotted carpet
baby in crib throws toy dog
pineapple juice in metal cup
spills, stiffens carpet in hot light.

Yellow kitchen yellow carpet
yellow light hot through bedroom window.

*

Nighttime quiet
quiet roomsounds
sounds far sounds close,
clock, housecreak
sad horn of passing train.

A mourning dove huHUs.
A Ferris wheel
out of control
one small boy
thrown out
over the city
but it's daytime
and he flies to the cul-de-sac
lands at the foot of his bed
east-facing summer morning.

*

Sounds in the house while it's still safe in the world.
Father in the kitchen eating yolks leaving whites.
Mother at coffee walking barefoot on terrazzo.

Sleep a partial shield thin but porous enough
to let through the steps, the plates, the boiling water,
light enough to slip back down to dreams.

And then melody and cadence fall away
until you realize you're padding the floors barefoot,
drinking coffee, guarding the morning and night
while someone else sleeps through your incidental fortress.

---

16   And if it's childhood then the ants are bright red, their bites sting
for hours. Bright red and crawling from volcanoes of tailings with no ideas,
no vessel to hold ideas, preparing for rain with no idea of rain. Ants on a white
vinyl chair in Pacific Grove, ants in file on pavements in Bagnone, ants in the
film by Buñuel and Dalí where the eye is sliced. Ants pressed into cheese in a film
called "Chocolate." Red ants. Black ants. Small ants. Ants in the underworld
where children dig and the stings last forever.

9

And now the daughter
off to the desert.

       (Rolling tape of road
       mountains clear and distant.)

A motel room
the smell of leaking stove.

       (Boulders aggregate to foothills
       sky black but warm.)

Like gold to airy thinesse beate.
What her skin will feel. What her eyes will see.

10

In summer lungs are sore
breathing round and painful
air thick enough to see.

There's a dream and you dream it.
It makes no difference how old you think you are.

Memory, dream: scant difference.

Set foot on the cul-de-sac
now a miniature set
the giants gone to grave,
and a wall of eucalyptus,
an orange grove, a missing list
of missing elders.

From yellow kitchen
a driveway, a street, the whole world
now a doll house, far, far away.

One day a green parakeet appears on the drive.
Its feet grip a young finger.
Manifestation? Messenger?
No one left to read the sign.

Seven Islands

1

The Isolato up from under
each sea a desert each moat a desert too.

And if time dissolves bridges or memories,
so moats, so oceans dissolve.

Birdsong and birds too high in the current
and curtains that billow into the room
these too islands, too deserts
that rise up at evening to greet you.

Atoll too a moat
dust motes too an archipelago.

2

But when the waters come, when the waters
from saturated air and over-laden clouds
unload in sheets and torrents
and the deepest valleys become the deepest seas
and rivers, lakes and moats overflow,
the struggle's dry against wet
warm body warm blood
against cold blood and gills;
those that fly or walk or crawl or slither
versus those that swim or drift or fix in place.[17]

---

17   "Senza fissarle / noi le liberiamo," Rabitti writes.

3

Isle of lost friends
not a step in a process,
by which I mean that ritual
and linked events may correlate
with causation in doubt.

The dark woods on the isle however
haunt and are haunted regardless.

4

The Isle of Lost Friends not where the lost friends are.
It's a marker, though; a placeless place.
It's not the *Commedia*, not a bus with no exit,
just a marker for the sorrows of time's ratchet.
There may be a forest there, a sheltered interior,
an isolated house surrounded by gum trees
but there's no way to a marker that's not also a place.

5

We hope our remnants will someday fit the puzzle.
The headlines shift like a weather horizon.

Some don't understand that collecting looks idle.
Maybe "combing" is a better verb
sifting the water's fringe.

Black basaltic outcrop
black waters and perfectly clear.
He combs the sand. She dives the reef.
They are the same person.
Sorting and collecting, combining and refiguring
as far from continents as the sphere allows.

If what you picture is warm and tropical
you're missing the point.
The barren, vast moat makes the attraction
not the metaphor, the drive not the symbol.

6

Water has no memory
memory no certain neuron
and yet continuity, and yet a memory of water.

Light is invisible, like wind, until it touches something.
Its impediments its history.

Rain and birdsong:
Dark, warm morning.

That a river was forgetting
and the walls surrounded by rivers
an unremembered city.

A brain spun of rivers
the city an island.

Water has no memory.

7

The poet arrives vocabulary ablaze
can't tell the difference between repetition and process.

The daughter across the table, on the floor drawing pictures.
Suddenly the daughter building the table.

The table an island.
Memory an island.

The City Revisited

1

Smoke blows away.
The city still standing.
Smoking boundary stones
a wall again, 30 feet tall.
Towers and citadels,
a city's busy motion
at war or at peace.

It doesn't last long, but savor what can be savored.
Call of crows, flash of wide black wings
and the whole thing's back to rubble
boundary stones cold and scattered, the city desert again.[18]
The ocean gone too, though you can feel its pulse
on the soles of your feet.

---

18   Islands of deserts and the ocean between them. Cities perched
on verges. Places sewn together by a single cartographer. The city verged and
planted; the keeper and destroyer; refiner and corrupter.

2

Water laps the city's steps;
steppes submerge in runoff.

We watch as wood burns
entrance ourselves with flame.
How could you see the world as I do?

Littered pavements
copper light before sun.
Birds singing for hours.

3

Akhilleus never enters the city
and Socrates never escapes it.

When the parts are few
easy to see where things align.

In the ideal city
the core is always tranquil

the light post-solstice, evenings quiet
like the core of a fortress city at war.

What to make of the city that executes its philosophers?
Or in the twilight tiny birds too high up in the current.

4

Feet on gravel
face flat on stone
a cartographer marks bend and rubble
neap and spring.

Trickle in the arroyo,
once a floodtide
that ripped aside the hero.

Is it a mirror reflecting moonlight ignites the sound of words?
Cartographer squints, sheds his calling:
from the far bank something almost tangible calls.

5

And people would say thereafter
how kindly they'd been treated
how leaving they'd been burdened with gifts
how hard it was to leave or stay, how difficult the road
the end of which was never achieved.
How distance doesn't narrow in the present.

6

Come to the gates amid unknown travelers[19]
the gatekeeper too just a vagrant.
If only there were a single word
for the known and the unknown.

The gatekeeper just another vagrant.
Sun increments north on the eastern scale
for the unknown and the known.
Chariots careen with or without wings.

Sun incrementing on scales imaginary.
They ask to enter but there are no gates.
Chariot, one way or another, slower than remembered.
The keeper among them.

They ask to enter but there are no gates.
Ordering coffee in a language they give him
the keeper absorbed among them
in shops suddenly material.

Coffee, tongues; given, received
trying to let go the voice that stops understanding
in shops suddenly material.
And when it's desert again

trying to release the voice that blocks understanding
and the clouds' shadows displace the city
and when it's desert again
the keeper no longer keeps anything.

As clouds' shadows presage the city
in the rising currents of his own memories
the keeper no longer keeps anything.
Dusk near again

fording the floodtide of his own memories
across a dark valley
toward the gated city's lights
for the known and the unknown.

---

19   Who knows when the gates will give way and voices pour
through the breech? A riot of voices ginned only in the brain. Tidal current of
voices. Automatic, ever-present voices.

Eleven-Part Treatise on Process

1

Meridians, latitudes, the sky crosshatched
but only on paper.

Whose poor language now? Or poor,
what do we call poor?

A map elemented,
bend of river, curve of bay, drift of continents,
isles continental and volcanic,
displacement of time rushing to the core.

Yet who can account for how gravity equals time
or the decisions people make?[20]

Let the curtains flow or the tiny birds too high in the current...
This the wanderer we live on.

Fleeting though one's judgment is and predictable.

Meridians? Latitudes? The sharp terraces of the Cinque Terre,
the rush of eclipse off North Kohala,
the lie the visitor tells herself,
the 10¢ peer into the future.
Hard to know the frame at these coordinates,
the pane gone dark
and we stuck bouncing echoes
from roof beams and floor joists
that actually cross hatch, actually bind.

There can't be a map without water.

*

A map, a taxonomy.
It's the groupings give pause
and each subset too.

---

20   Whose legends mark the unmarkable? Time and space are not a
trampoline, and yet the metaphor barely clears things up.

Is it the definition of insanity
to make a map and remake a map?

The metamorphic nature of fire
the liquid nature of flame.

And yet this morning's overcast tinges green
almost the undertone of a bruise,
almost the locked door of sleep unlocked,
deserted then guarded
on a boulevard that makes no waking sense.

Yet not all proofs of waking obtain.

Let the applicant remember what the job is.

2

Ghost in the curtains ghost in the machine.
The world's full of wonders
and if I say the trees and leaves are animated
what soul should I ascribe to the wind
or what then has agency?

Leaf shadows playing on windows,
wet leaves glinting in sunlight
are themselves enough.

You might record the voices of the dissolve into sleep
or hear them enough to remember the tone if not the words,
the music if not the language.

3

A dream of masks and what makes a mask
a masque of a dream and what music makes a masque.

Understanding that fragments and shards cohere
whose voice do you hear approving or disapproving?
Whose voice approaching or disappearing?

A hat or a mask, a wig or a mask
a suit or a mask, a masque or a mask.

The blue buzz too high up in the current a masque.

*

Leave the bark anothered
a masque.

Whaling ship: same problem.

Array the spirits on the island
vengeance, retirement, hope, surrender
and O, or ah, the ability to do it.

To people else the isle
with units of integrity.

4

That you would come to a shore
a shore of rock and sand
a shore of tile and city steps
far beyond the horizon.

Someone says "This is no way to escape the desert
because you can't escape the desert."

*

Islands of deserts and the ocean between them.
Cities perched on verges
places strung together by a single cartographer
the city perched and planted
the keeper and destroyer,
refiner and corrupter.

*

The broken frame, the scattered cups,
remnants in wind and dust.
Sand everywhere.

Water lapping the main street
but sea water not sweet water
and wind and wood, sand in the creases,
horizon duned, horizon rimmed by mountain range,
basins, empty basins
but the ocean, the persistent, thoughtless ocean
intruding because this map slaps the seawall,
the ancient steps, the dooryard's font
the thoughtless ocean, lined and colored,
simpler and more complex
with every mark, with every agitation.

5

Waiting for an emissary the world's full of emissaries waiting for
a story instead and the emissary an actor or insect lighter than air,
coral insects combing depths in heavier atmospheres each column
weighing down on the messengers the messages squeezed thin and
indecipherable like *gold to airy thinesse beate.*

Waiting for the currents to lift them high too high in the currents
and the tiny birds circling too high in the currents emissaries in
circuit too high in the cycle too high in the sphere.[21]

So light goes silver the blue grey sky goes amotion.

---

21   As if we actually had winters, and the sun slid so far south it's
past the window especially on a barge mid-ocean where there are no windows,
but still, a steel sky and pavements piled with leaves, what would it be like to
retire from writing?

6

And the world that disappears
with the return of serotonin.

Or the world that vanishes at the end of the story.

And Akhilleus who never enters the city
asleep in his well-built shelter
and Stephen who walks off in a predawn June
a ghost without a citadel.[22]

---

22   The way shadows moving on a window's screen can seem cool
or warm by the frequency of their tremors; by excrescence, unfurling in
cell and field, by rivers filling valleys, and I don't mean anything pathological,
I mean the unfurling, budding, flowering, metamorphic nature of things.

7

She asks where the dream when the dream's lost its code.
We'll leave the argument for later, maybe for history.
She or he claims chemistry and mechanical function.
He or she says all people from all times; the Hero, C.J. Jung.

We'll set the argument aside for now. History takes care of itself.
After all, if even a sentence is a narrative, why not?
Someone looking for continuity says, all people, all times, Jung, Heroes
and we're left to wonder whether their versions of the story obtain at all.

After all, sentence or sequence or line up against the wall,
why exclude even the most vivid dream, at least as record?
And we'll not be left to wonder about stories obtaining
let alone a code in need of a codebook.

Resolved to include even the most vivid dream just for the record
or to study how one Viennese sought to merge science and myth.
As for a code in need of a code book, forget it,
it's the brain awash in chemistry, not missives from the great ocean.

We'll leave the argument aside for now; even a sentence, etc.
And she asks when the dream, then the code, then the story's lost?

8

Who knows when the gates will give way
and voices pour through the breech?

A riot of voices ginned in the brain.

The flood of voices.
The automatic, always present voices.

*

Hot light, low angle.
Just look up from the paper.
Forget the index.

*

Who was running who was chaste
Daphne one lifetime ago
laurel enough for working

then explain the simultaneous
speeding and slowing of age
the mystery of voicings
the archive evanescent.

*

But by starting where the voices are fresh
and maybe fresh means morning
or maybe, simply, starting over,
hearing what can be heard,
then telling it, regathered,
voiced, sounded, measured out again.

9

And so the cartographer makes the map once more.

The scales are never the same,
the approaches and projections array.

The work is never complete,
the charts are never quite right.

The cartographer's aware of this problem.[23]
In the end, says the cartographer,
even taken together, the whole will be incomplete.
That is my vocation.

---

23   Mid winter, university library, the cartographer down to stacks
lit by timers, basement windows pelted with rain; cold air, cold metal shelves.
Somewhere, cooled on steel, in that see, kleos enough.

10

Sitting by fire the cartographer watches meat grill.
Crepuscle impinging, the cartographer marks flame and light.
Call this a season, the legend notes, cross-hatching an aura
we might call climate.

Observed from afar, the cartographer may appear listless, but this
is not the case.

A cartographer's pause allows geology to settle,
for tectonic plates to subduct, for mammals to hide fingers in
pectoral fins, for tails to retract to coccyxes.

11

The cartographer is tired and still the world appears to change.
The burdened, dormant desk, the drawn and re-drawn lines,
the separated continents, the elements that want to congeal to mass
and those that actually can; the task, the folly, the center that holds.

Still, in an eye's blink,
below a bowsprit not seen before,
faster than time allows,
three sirens appear then vanish
and the ship they rode on.

"Dream's transom," marks the cartographer
who, dreaming, battles foe familiar and strange
to awake with regret and hope, but without memory.

Ten Attitudes (with Water)

1

Watching water well in the vessel
wondering why we script the scenes as we do
thinking surely something must have been learned.[24]

---

24   Across a wide plane upheaval of mountains, eruptions of lore. Long
shadows, deep shadows, the region's bare and rocky ranges, a silence so filigreed
it's noisy. By which the growing drought's invoked, the gradual disappearance of
water, the desert's reclamation. The transformation to something almost verdant
just a temporary relaxation of gravel, sand, and waterless wind.

2

Yet with or without water
it's the shadows, long and deep
magnetic shadows
in the winter's angle
that haunt the landscape
that pull the fixed eye.

The fixed eye pulled,
the long, thoughtless gaze.

3

Water has no memory.
Memory's only seat has no specific neuron.
And yet continuity, and yet a memory of water.

Wind like light's invisible without contact.
Its collisions its history.

Dark, warm morning: Rain
and birdsong.

No accident that a river was forgetting.

What mother bathed her child there
no heel left unwashed?

A world of water, a brain spun of rivers,
a continent riven by them.

Water has no memory.

4

Dead fish under metal grid and rats
how did the pool drain so quickly?

Boys at the lane lines—they're all you!—
counting the hours till their shift is done.
They may or may not effect a rescue
but off-duty, when the customers are gone
the water roils and swells
and who are you if not the one to swim through it
but that the water suddenly drains away.

You can dive through the gap at the pool's bottom
and climb to safety past the rat and fish remains,
past carnivorous snails with stretching antennae
but that's not remotely the issue.

5

Cobbles, water, beckoning hands.
Pulling for the far bank and signal fires
we yearn for the ferryman. We get the flood.

Stretching hands. Cobbles and cataracts.
The far bank farther in flood.
We yearn for the ferryman, the signal fire.

6

Polish the corner. *Riverrun.*
Who swims the current, who's already across?
On the bank opposite, one more figure signals with fire.

Back at sea, the cartographer goes to the wheelhouse.
X degrees of separation, feet on the console,
long, numb stretches of time
then boom—an island, a reef,
a tanker passing too close.

7

The cartographer, saddened, abjures the wheelhouse.
Steering not a cartographer's job.
Governors use different methods.

Ants parade on a trail of pheromones
mapless, unguided, at sea without allegory.

8

Feet on gravel
face flat on stone
cartographer marks bend and scrabble
neap and spring.

In the arroyo a trickle once a floodtide
washing even the toughest aside.

Is it a mirror reflecting moonlight
ignites at the sound of words?
The cartographer squints, sheds his calling.
From the far bank something almost tangible calls.

9

Ferryman closer than the chart records.
Cartographer factors the grief time induces.

Dog paws drag across the bank's alluvium.

The ferryman pauses, uncertain of his mandate.
All that live die, but who's allowed to board?

The cartographer's compass also unclear:
topography alone can't answer the charge.[25]

Being and nothingness someone called it.
The alluvia, the ferry's hull, the instruments of mapping.

Pasadena 2017–2025

---

25   Fire, reflection, dust in the wind.